GALOS; Z J

LOVE & ART

SONGS OF PASSION

Second Volume

Poetry & Drawing

Impressum

Bibliographical information of the German National Library. The German National Library indexes this publication with the German National Bibliography. Detailed bibliographical data may be derived from the Internet website: hpp://dnb.dnb.de

First Revised Edition October 2024
©2024 Z J GALOS
©2024 Cover art and drawings: z. galos
©2024 Cover design: jan ateet frankl

Publisher: BoD · Books on Demand GmbH, In de Tarpen 42, 22848 Norderstedt
Print: Libri Plureos GmbH, Friedensallee 273, 22763 Hamburg

ISBN: 978-3-7597-8856-6

"Every heart sings a song, incomplete, until another heart
Whispers back. Those who wish to sing always find a song.
At the touch of lovers, everyone becomes a poet."

Plato

"One day you will ask me which is more important? My life or
yours? I will say mine and you will walk away not knowing you
are my life."   Khalil Gibran

"Love is an irresistible desire, to be irresistibly desired."

Robert Frost

Prolog

Love & Art's Second Volume, with its drawings conceived during a workshop in the suburb of Voula, in Athens, during an art workshop for local and foreign artists who communicated through their art. The space, rented by a doctor, entailed a space for an administration office, a corner with a bar and some barstools at a higher area, and a more expansive space suitable for a small stage for theatre and entertainment purposes. The white walls were used to exhibit unknown and known local and foreign artists who participated in workshops and joined the small group of local artists. The atmosphere radiated good vibes from the owner and his friends, who met there regularly.

Artistic communication stimulated my inner chords for notations and sketches, which I often immediately transferred into poems, mostly love poems. A dusky woman of great animalistic radiance moved like a cat between our drawing tables and inspired, painted in quick successions her canvases. The first workshop became a roaring success for artists and visitors alike. I brought my concept drawings, prepared canvases, and worked eagerly from day one. The owner had invited an established artist from Zagreb, who commented on our work and offered discussions about art. I had already developed my style, and most of the time, he had some pointers for me about painting techniques. Still, in art, I had my road mapped ahead and behaved quite stubbornly about my perspective of how I saw my results on my canvases, watercolours, and drawings.

Having successfully finished the art workshop, I met a sensuous Muse who became my model and inspiration for most of these love poems. This inspired me to follow up on the poetry of the art workshop's cat woman, Eva. Jo, Maria, and Val all inspired me with their coarse, different female attributes and interest in contemporary art.

The poems were written into my cerise-coloured ciak art journal, which I acquired in a stationary shop in Ermou Street; it entails 91 poems with equally as many drawings of the 230-page art book, filling 169 pages, with 61 pages still empty for perhaps a future continuation. As I like reducing numbers, 169 =7, and so does 61. As I have written 91 poems, they are reduced to 10 =1, precisely the reduction of my birthday. Interesting? I love to do that!

Written in 10 months, between September 2006 and July 2010, it gives an inside view of those times and reflects an excellent jouissance.., for the artist and the poet in the dialogue of love and art.

*

LOVE & ART

The Passionate Dialog

nyx

life's dusk that catches me
a police car's siren that cuts into
the stillness of the night
like exploding fireworks
from streetfighters
a taxi mini cab takes revenge
on a bus.
the week's tiredness inundates me
with bombs detonating
challenging an iron hand of a
strong leader
not yet has he emerged in front
of all our eyes
thanatos has copied herself many
times to lie with nyx, queen of
the night
besides the jealous pairing of
darkness and sleep –
erebus and hypnos –
challenging sweet eros who rules
over your sensual demeanour
I always crave for, I always want.

L&A II drwg.01 (28) – nyx

night's heaven

you lead me into the world
of your love
    that took me on its silver beam
into the shadows of the universe
    filled with an abundance of
the spirits of the night
    a milky nyx from the dust of chaos
absorbed by the deity of darkness
    she parades her offspring:
aether on a cloud of oneiroi
    where momus reigns and ponos
toils blaming him for all the hard work
    of gathering all the ungraspable air
and thanatos visits on a black float
    hynos, her sister of death
fast asleep on a ferry of mummed
    deceased, charon steers the silent
boat of the night's heaven on an
    odyssey across the dark-blue seas
you kiss me, hug me tightly as heaven
    glows in the colours of the new-born
day where eris fights at the side of
    nemesis and apate
deceives them with her cunning
    strategies, but we join philotes
joining nyx's daughter who holds
    the mirror of eros
who has magically absorbed in
    both of us.

L&A drwg 02 (29) 2 – night's heaven

I thought of you

upside down, I sailed around you
sailing across your skin
diving into your sea of love
you have opened up for me
on this long journey, I have
embarked upon.
this adventure of words
I have played like a quiz
to place together for me
finding the sacred stone of happiness
that built itself up in my mind
over time, a burning torch, once set
on fire will light the way along
the darkened nights
you've cast magical clues as a
white cotton thread
that'll lead me from this labyrinth
of demons to the light of a new world
surrounded by hues of blue.
I thought of you as a sculpted nude
afloat, we dive for the isle below
the hearts that only talk.

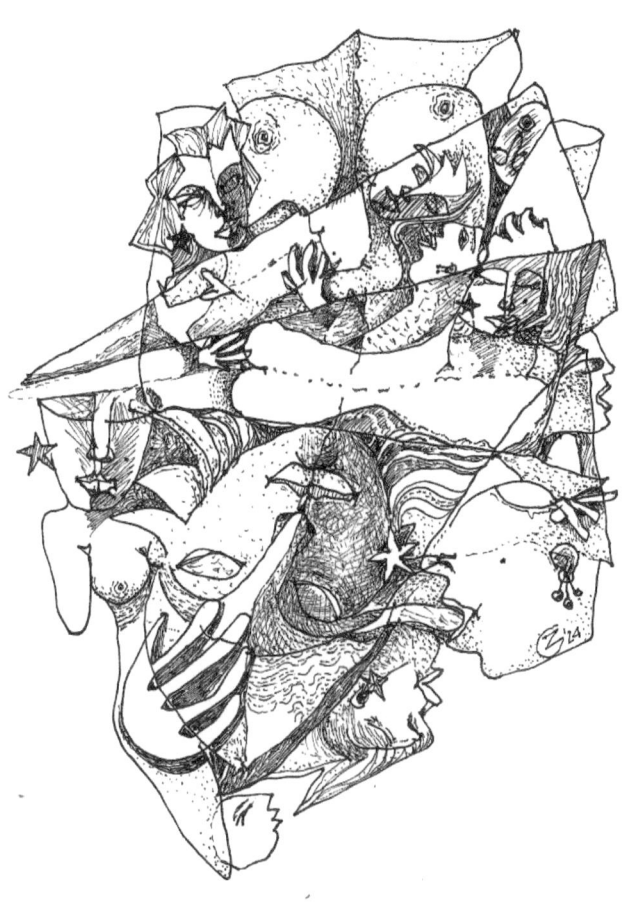

L&A II drwg 03 (30) – I thought of you

centrifuge of merging

you could read my inflamed mind
immediately
burn my shirt, my pants
denude me in a whirlwind touch
of senses
open the furnace door of love
meltdown my innermost core
to this heap of ashes
I reshape with my fingers
that dance and grow into the
new man who took off
white-winged and gleaming
like liquid leads to seeking your
touches that will reshape him
into the other part of you
you held into the purifying fires
to burn him into immortality
reunify the god-given spirit
with the warmth of humanity
the celestial dance of endless wheels
of the heavens
that turn man's fate in a centrifuge's
merging.

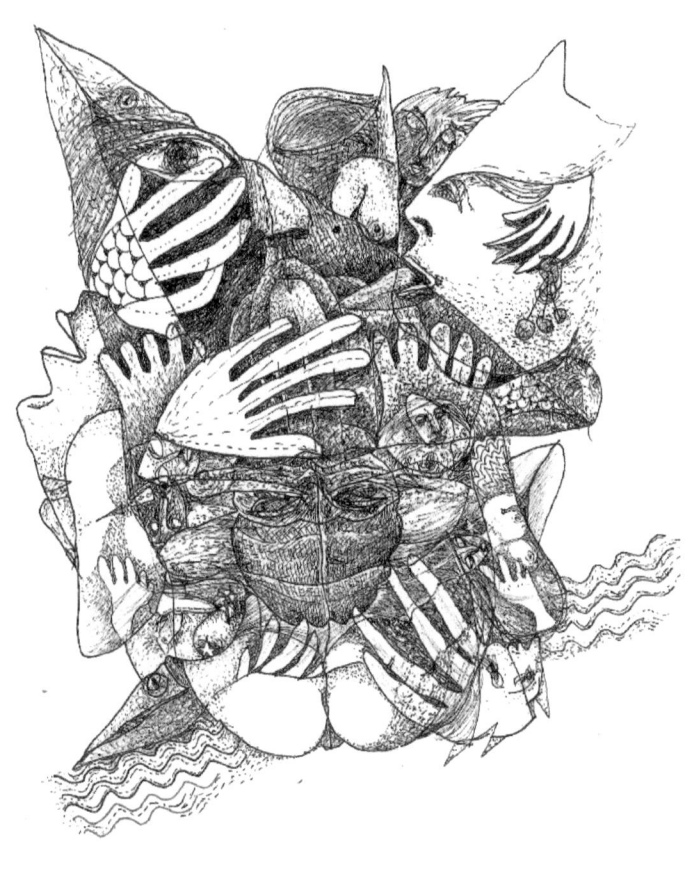

L&A II drwg 04 (31)– centrifuge of merging

body of marble

this body of marble
greatest art in sculpture
identity of a human
warmth of its skin
closeness with touch
sensation and body-longing
desires that do not see
physical destructions:
the missing of an arm
and a foot
the inspired physique that
grows back in love
comes alive with desire
and enriches one's being
not even a living thing
could provide
in such an instant embrace
that cuts out the critical mind
for the benefit of an
emotional intelligence
passionate exchanges
merging of most tender flesh
a union of unusual intensity
and longing
that sprung from the touch
of the marble's smooth body
a sculpture of the highest art.

L&A II drwg.05 (32) – body of marble

lustful fete

the first light hushes over
your marble body I have dug
from the dark shadows of
another night
cleaned from the flow of my
excitement
polished your thighs and torso
embraced those generous breasts
rolled you over to stroke along
your spine's sensual groove
until you woke with a sigh and
pulled me close
my finger stuck in your folds
my kisses, heaving your breasts
my hands mould you like dough
from a softly lit statue, eros leaped
and danced with us at a feast
of heaven' slide
we rolled in and out of our bodies
new-born at this lustful fete.

L&A II drwg.06 (33) – lustful fete

stealthy sacred rites

you left on the early boat
that rose to the heavens
and vanished in the mist
of a mid-september morn'.
I felt I had lost you to some
corny constellations
some velvet stout of feelings
that welled up in me.
I've drunk your mother's milk
yet you are still a woman without
eternal ties, without an offspring
but the one we have created in
our minds
searching in earth's bowels for
an answer, or a clue where to
place the next step in researching
the netherworld, the galleries of
passion and human suffering
that binds the erotic and the
spiritual worlds
we seek to explore together
in stealthy secret rites.

L&A II drwg.07 (34) – stealthy sacred rites

sparkling night

your mind and mine have
created many scenes
floating about in space
projecting great compositions
of our bodies in the playful
garden along helios' eternal ride
that lights up the nocturnal
dance of spirits and sculpts with
an instant chisel of rays
most magnificent marble statues
that freeze in the sharp play
of shadow and light
until we meet and kiss them
into life
until our touches and licks
will stir them up
until the erotic wheel of the
heavens will start to spin into
another sparkling night.

L&A II drwg.08 (35) – sparkling night

I miss you

Sailing above the
cumuli cloud towards
a land once enriched
by celebratory music
sweetened life with
sacher compositions
host to the cognisanti
literati, like zweig, kraus
schnitzler, and canetti
many others, from strauß
to mahler and berg
you mingle with the traditional
crowd where you've disappeared
into and I miss you as much as
seeking to share with you
the têtê-á-têtê's happy hours
the lover's talk, the banter, and
the stirring to build up to a
physical crescendo
the daily burn of lust we share
the pleasure of healthy laughs.

L&A II drwg.09 (36) – I miss you

shell

   I woke in the middle of
the night
   you breathe like a gasping fish
swallowing line, hook, and sinker
   of love's excitement
a lusting act of devouring
   a feeling of bewilderment
barefoot in underwear on a dusty
   road
eyes opened up wide in shock
   looking at a ruin
a burned-out middle section of
   the house I've lived with a spouse
a sweetheart and a family
   who are no longer present.
I err along in the distance, seeking
   your love and comfort in a
southern climate
   living off the deep blue sea's fruit
chew an olive and roll the spread out
   rocks to assemble a wall and cover
the light-flooded place with canalit
   that juts away over the barren cliff
challenging the heated air, the sounds
   of the sea caught in its shell.

L&A II drwg.10 (37) – shell

aphrodite's dance

in the lair of hades
the door opens for you
to arrange floating bodies
shards of marble and body parts
to a desired composition
in a tumble of giant faces, arms,
fingers, and legs that form
triangulated funnels
into which you'll arrange
the nubile girl, the sensual
southern woman, long-haired
aphrodite, point-headed nefertiti
and giant fingers on hugely-shaped
breasts, the time is soon up
when this creative composition
will take to life like a giant machine
an enormous wheel of the heavens
sailing from sun signs to moon signs
turning on the planetary dance
of the nightly heaven you dance with
and your body starts melting
in a hot, excited flow, you cast and
honour aphrodite's dance.

L&A II drwg.11 (38) – aphrodite's dance

caraway seed

this bone I chew is in my mind
and not a bone but my inflated libido
    pushing itself into a phallus
that you have clasped with a curled
    finger, a fist, and slipped your
hungry lips over
    wet and warm, you'll entice me
to the hilt, or could I still make it to
    the top of these attic hills
along the ceremonial way
    we've chosen as our high point
of celebration?
    this phallic wonderland of great
stimulation you wish to bring forth
    the same way I want to crawl
upon you sliding and clawing
    onto your hills and into your
valleys falling on earth's reverberating
    lust
we, as children of aphrodite carry in us
    like caraway seed.

L&A II drwg.12(39) – caraway seed

white roses

they are not solely soul sisters
but my muses, too much entangled
in white roses
for love between sisters is as pure as
the marble's white skin
that percolates its warmth into the
fingertips of desire's electrical spark
the triad has found its secret of stirring it
into creative configurations of body parts
in embraces and the flow of continual
reshaping the processional ritual
of love's many ways
from one corner of life's temple
in a frieze that depicts their erotic stories
I'm invited to join in at times with the
sensual *shy*, who hides between the other
two, but then it's *aggro* who attacks me
like an amazon, yet *sweet* is there all over me
to heal the pounding wounds of eros'
overflowing gifts falling like petals from the
white roses
they have held close between them.

L&A II drwg.13 (40) – white roses

faces

life's assembly of faces
along its processional frieze
the temple's outer face had faded
once the pride of a goddess
her appearance to the outer world
torn apart by men's greed and
primordial drive for possession
as if ideas in the abstract could ever
be acquired by ripping off the
depicted celebration, destroying fine art
chip off its marbles transformed into
god-like shapes and an appearance
as life is nothing more than
continuous strives of aggression out of
caves
the artist assembles the smallest pebble,
the least of shards
and recreates life beyond destruction
the poet longs to end the
philosophers weeping about it.

L&A II drwg.14 (41) - faces

love & art

    from the nocturnal travels
through my conscious
    have I touched the greatness
of minds from Leonardo to lempicka
    picasso to chagall
have rubbed upon their genius
    my body, a flowing fountain pen
pushing upon pages of virgin paper
    urging my innerness to recreate
the myriad of feelings and emotions
    all the greatest stirs in the poet's soul
words fall like dew onto the waking day
    lines rustle upon the skin
the artist will catch to reshape
    creation in a continuation of merging
emotions
    and celebrating love
that is the greatest art.
    love & art.tra & evol

L&A II drwg. 15(42) – love & art

burn of point relief

    suspended in the air of insouciance
we touch as if by accident floating objects
    our bodies in the hourglass of time
hearts beating in expectation for the renewal
    of a free and most exciting life ahead
at the dawn of earth's raging fires that
    passion has ignited over a thousand
têtê-á-têtê's, with thousands of touches
    never tiring lips of licking the devouring
mouths that greedily sweep across
    boiling skins, the flowing sea of juices
love has in its generosity and dire need
    blessed lovers with
bestowed on them
    the burn of point relief.

A&L II drwg 16 (43) – burn of point relief

upside down

behind the frieze of marbled veils
we touch, we venerate each other
offer this suspended love
this lone walk to boy electronic
this burning body flow of our juices
into the most incredible merging of them all
into the hot air of the singing rock
the spring of life that cleans the body
and purifies the soul into the
marble pieces we hug and slide upon
the art we have embraced in
palimpsest movements
the minds have dictated for thousands
of years, but we have detected this great dig
since the stars fell burning the
olive groves, torturing the land
like love tortures the skin and pushes up
ravines in eruptive desires
turning the body's undulations
upside down.

L&A II drwg 17(44) – upside down

projections of the soul

onto the curvatures of giant
marble art we project the show
we've recorded inside our souls
merged into this classical art in a new
expressive way
the gentle flight of your senses with
the colours of the sea
that changes like the mood of lovers
and from the flight of nudes
the red-hot sun of creation chases
you with my desires that lay you
across this raft of a foam-swept love
moving in a slow dance
with our bodies synced in the ways
we fit together, as in making love
the wave of great lust's compositions
in hellenistic art taken to the
spread-eagled stretches of
materialized words
where thoughts are rhythmic pulsations
the musical ecstasy
living out our wildest dreams
at an instant.

L&A II drwg 18(45) – projections of the soul

arrow's head

I transformed from above
to below at the drop of a hat
     my funds have been taken
with a bleep to publish *spleen of love*
     much faster than we could say
hello or stroke and kiss, exchange
     our blood.
you have morphed into aphrodite
     venerated by you and me as
beloved mother of naughty eros
     who changes hearts at will with
his magical bow and arrow
     hardly missing his target
deeper into our bodies every time
     we meet and kiss, and we touch
to let desires creep all over our
     clasping hearts
the gasps we both fall into
     opened up by the erotic child's
deep penetrating arrowhead.

L&A II drwg.19 (46) – arrow's head

art's greatest past

    from praha to yerewan
from Belarus to Beijing
    your bevy of most loyal friends
will entice the body's longing
    but only in the mind and desire
the same kind of sexually fulfilled life
    as I have encountered in the city
of athens, where statues of great art
    if not the greatest, turn into the
love of your life
    demanding the complete transformation
of body and soul, a breakdown of one's
    existence into the kits of parts, just like
the shards of marble that once have been
    strewn over the top of the acropolis
were painstakingly assembled back again
    despite explosions, barbaric acts, and
due to the vagaries of the gnawing teeth
    of time, all men fight, all women herd up
against and like the poet, who follow
    their sacred call of the innermost –
love will be the greatest weapon,
    the catalyst that'll reshape
art's greatest past.

L&A II drwg 20 (47) – art's greatest past

intimate clasp

    your embrace hastens my speed
of rushing blood
    screaming along my arms and legs
grows my phallus into you
    like the winding vine into the
marble column you slide upon
    in visions of great lust for all's
substance and all's come alive in
    the warmth of your hand's caresses
the clasp that wakes up life
    the probing finger that slips along
your wetted folds, not satisfied, until it
    penetrates all slits and holes
like a herald calls for a feast of senses
    its head red and blown up to its
loveable size, it's drawn to merge
    the juices of life, the kiss of the
unfurling rose of your cunt
    its intimate clasp that we desired
to last.

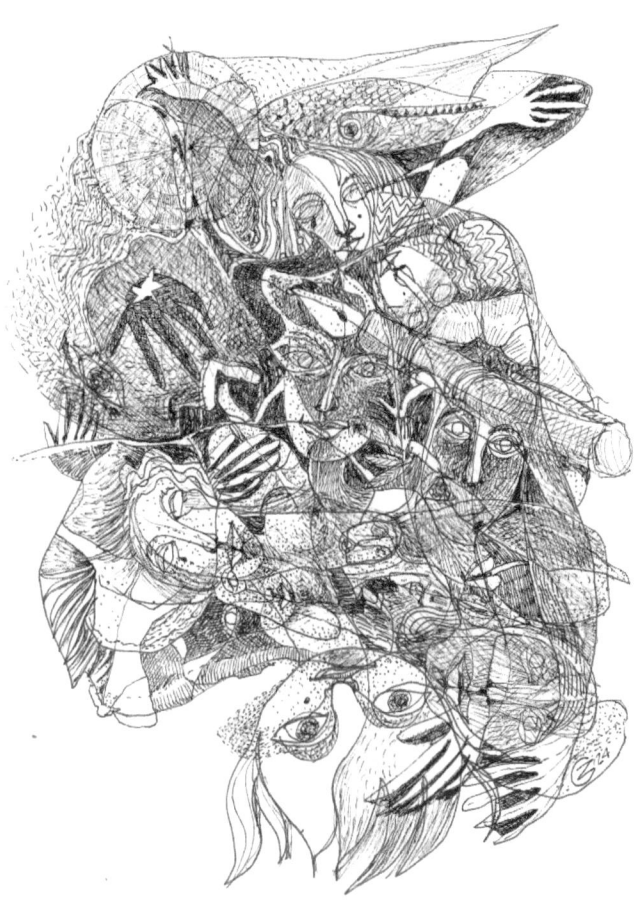

L&A II drwg.21 (48) – intimate clasp

ballast of passion

   you tell me endearments
send me love notes and I realize
   in a countdown for love's long
awaited meeting
   with images, you and I have called up
in our dialogues
   your breasts' shape are heavenly cushions
will absorb my fall upon you
   in the heat that leads to our first
hungry erotic exchanges you encourage me
   to sail on your body's shell out to sea
chose a love-inducing island that'll turn us
   into its sole inhabitants
your nude and mine I'll draw and paint
   a holistic depiction of love's
multifaceted feelings
   the up-and-down climb on the ladder
of lust, caresses that curl and stretch
   kisses that suck up every drop of the
fiery liquid we douse each other with
   marinate our skins
dive like dolphins
   playing amongst the fish, and I toss
the ballast of passion deep into you.

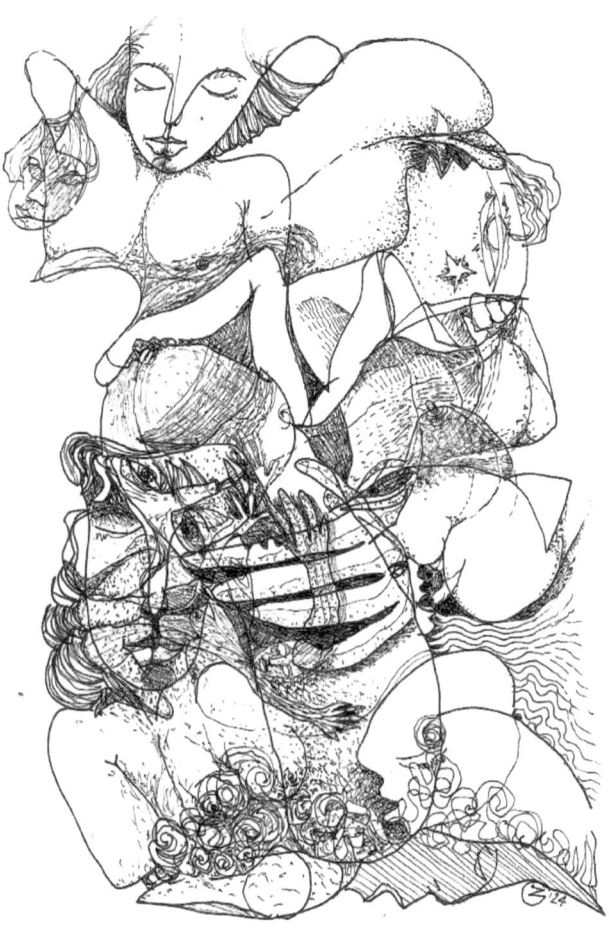

L&A II drwg.22 (49) – ballast of passion

libido's greatest rise

on the stones, time tread upon
haphazardly
    I see your portrait come alive
my hands intuitively wave and dance
    an artist's brush, assembling, changing
rearranging colourful lines and bouquets
    of stone flowers tied up with a
vibrant life
    as if life's giant sundial had assembled
for thousands of years
    yet nobody touched the magic stones
the playful rays that light up if all's stroked
    the right way in a pleasure ride
a rebirth of your erotic being
    a great merging of minds that'll live on
in my accidental compositions, you have
    a finger in, a hand, an arm, a torso with
desirable bosom, an expressive derriere
    that twists and bends in great excitement
sucking in any libido's greatest rise.

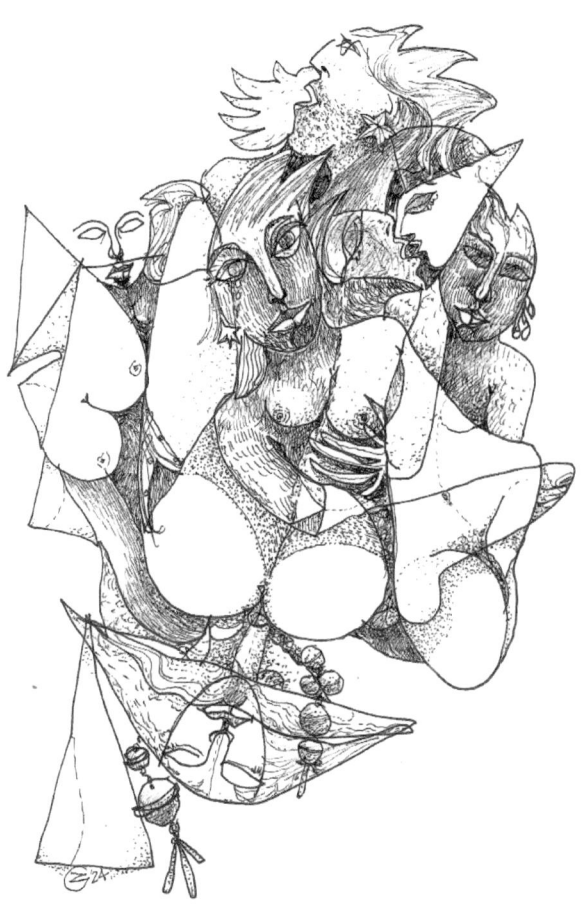

L&A II drwg.23 (50) – libido's greatest rise

celebrating love

    lost in the lines
I draw your finger in mine
    that shapes your body
onto the page
    my fingers holding your body
my inner child at play
    discovers your bodylines
I grow into you like the vines
    along the terrace beams
that shade the place of our
    close togetherness – this illusion
alive within my mind, I've lost the
    thread of safety that will lead me
to the light of a new day and a new
    beginning of grasping my lines
I draw with the same longing
    a potter shapes his vases anew
while I feast on the shards of my
    imagination
celebrating love.

L&A II drwg. 24 (51) – celebrating love

fading hope

for the first time, I could not
wait for you to come online
    for an intimate tête-á-têtê
I would need dearly after a week
    of abstinence
my body's purple and red
    blossoming with flowers
that looked like tattoos
    imprinted by my acts of
autoerotic love – it indicated
    my state of e-life suffered
since you've left
    the airlines are now carriers of
goods and do not care particularly
    about their passengers
treating them like numbers
    a lifeload of chicken.
I had a rough time getting to you
    feeling you, kissing you
with the magic fizzed out and
    disappointments mounting
hindrances of meeting you are
    continuing albeit my constant
efforts to overcome pecuniary
    obstacles, a see-saw love life
a long-haul flight to athens
    fading hope with a walk to the
middle of the bridge
    that cracks up in an earthquake.

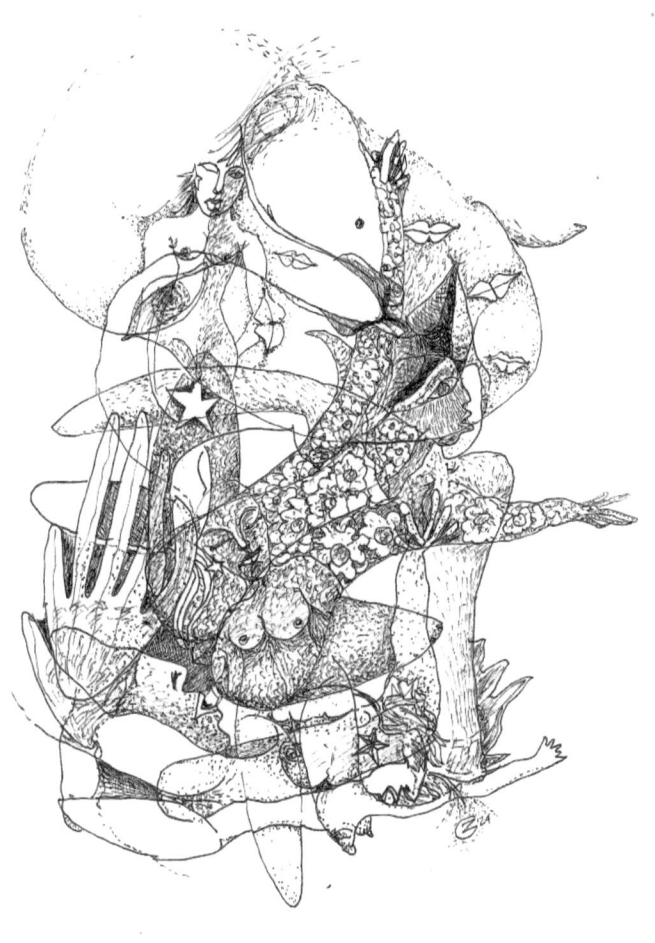

L&A II drwg. 25 (52) – fading hope

stealthy love exploding?

yesterday's tardy libido woke up
today to your tease, to your body,
　your torso you show me
opened up below your zipped-open
　bath coat
arousing my lust to hold you
　push myself as a whole onto your
body, between your full breasts and
　closer to you pushing your feet apart
you speak of being bad once in a while
　otherwise decent to do it behind
the paravent of keeping a face for the
　public – you are quite right, nothing
could destroy one's love faster than
　the wide open mouth of gossip.
I draw you behind the curtain behind
　the doors that lead to the inner
sanctum of the chapel-
　I show you the doors where I spent
excitement with embraces of
　stealthy love exploding behind.

L&A II drwg.26 (53) – stealthy love exploding

his mind's oracle

in the ocean of touches
and warm bodies
my libido thrives in your rich
passionate offerings to hold me
high above the ground of strife
and maiming wars
that started in troja and since
have been copied in continuous
succession and at one time
everybody who has feet will run
the walls around the golden city
will fall just like the walls at jericho
zeni will slip into the silver bird
of sleek and sonic speed that would
be recognizable rather as an escape
than a trojan horse
he'll wander to eleusis
seek a love that will be hekate,
demeter, and persephone in one
in one woman promised to him
by his mind's oracle.

L&A II drwg. 27 (54) – his mind's oracle

I look for her

and the dusky woman
fruit of cocoa and the scent of
cinnamon
spreads her warm island smile
I paint her like gauguin in the midst
of sandstone hills and olive trees for
shade
she lies spread-eagled for her continuous
love affairs, like earth-mother embracing
everybody who comes close to her
fascinated by her racy features
her broad-shouldered chiselled body
I brush onto my canvas, or so it appears
to me as I browse thru' a tour of my other
life, I left behind
the crying gaps between the ancient stones
of the mighty temple and david appears
like an actor on stage
anna smiles as she strips for my eyes
forever a youtube-clip she sent me
in between the shards I look for her
the marbled flutes
the palimpsest strokes of
greatest art.

L&A II drwg. 28 (55) – I look for her

waking lewdness

    to the sound of flight
the hum of a thousand songs
    the chafing wind speeds with
its icy grip along the cigar-shape
    of the body of the plane
your thoughts flow in a tight sheaf
    on me
the play of piano fingers, tapping feet
    that clasp my waist, my hip
my flying arms, my waiving feet
    for the cushioned breasts with
their pointed nipples like two studs
    ripping along my skin
zip me loose from any heavy
    earthliness
to the clouds, the stars, a new day
    breaking up the hours of
merging shadows
    that flee like forbidden dreams
of waking lewdness.

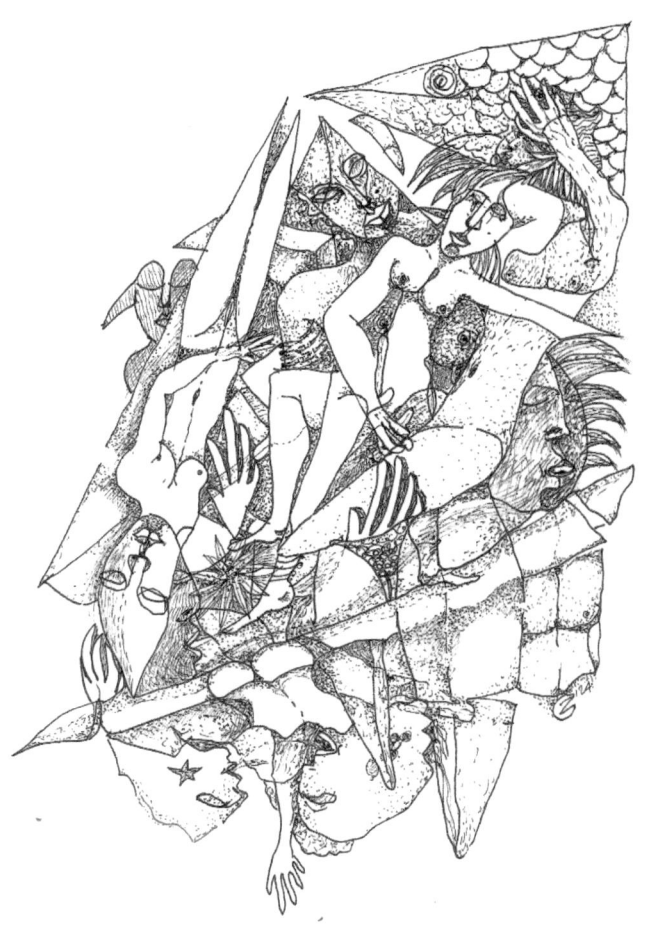

L&A II drwg. 29 (56) – waking lewdness

human need (day one)

you move with mechanical
ability, oiled, and at speed
    I dare to intercept with friendly
kisses on your cheeks and the words
    that percolate quickly
speedily tossed between gasps for
    more tightly embraces
a deeper penetration for the sexual
    hunger that sears between the looks
and gestures, the polite and
    animated talk of greeks
I'm becoming a greater part of
    and I feel to absorb the places
I loved all my life thru' you
    I see in front of me: acropolis, NAM
the lysikrates monument, the plaka's
    polished cobblestone road where
the feet feel at home and welcomed
    directed to friends and people
we know for many years in our lives
    their warm smile, shaking hands
the quaint ritual of a new but ever
    present life, the other life
the human need.

L&A II drwg.30 (57) – human need

art that swallowed me up (day two)

though art' you now?
where are you sprung from?
   As from the artful shards of
poros marble
   luminous and smooth
alive with the eyes of a sphinx
   lips curled to an archaic smile
everybody stands at her feet
   to admire its innate happiness
we all wish to have and share
   we all strive to reach that level
where mind and soul celebrate
   the being's awareness
as we arrive at the pearly gate of
   self-realization.
where art' you now my mate of
   soul? woman with the mind of
a sphinx?
   I've searched the worldwide net
found the sixth caryatid crying
   like the face that became the
worldwide expression of sorrow
   and pain I've drawn onto my
pages of the acropolis museum's
   guide for the floors of art
that swallowed me up.

L&A II drwg. 31 (58) – art that swallowed me up

for the first time (day three)

I drive with you in your
smooth sounding car
   my hands wish to be on you
   like yours in on the steering wheel
my body you steer with your
fingers clasping my thighs
   your kisses are warm and luscious
   like your body's fruit
I want to dive into and
you dive into me from the top of the roof
   between the sunshade's gab
   I feel your wet and succulent arousal
the more we dig into each other
the more we thrive on top of the soul
   the flight of excitement will take us
   to the top and beyond the city's
pebble-shard-lines of streets and
buildings we land on the sacred rock
   I love you on me and I on you
   we'll rock each other in continuous
succession: ena, dhio, tria...I count
as you teach me in the fresh waves of
   thalassa we touch, we kiss like
   innocent children
for the first time.

L&A II drwg. 32 (59) – for the first time (day three)

enter paradise (day four)

three nights in glyfada
between the soft-green pines
the distance of a few roads
you drive me, my hand on your
thigh, my blood that boils and
sprays its white drops all over
your cheeks and lips
dissolving like pearls rolling down
caressing your breasts with an
instant urge to dig deeper into you
feel my throbbing heart on their
red-brown tips
spread across your lips, your thighs
your sweet luscious lips that open
below to draw me in and dip into
your sea of love to jump in joy and
to move in unison
back and forth
forth and back
your gasps I want to heighten
and be in your front and back
fingers, lips, and tongue
and one more time
front and back
front and back
and pushing hard to
enter paradise.

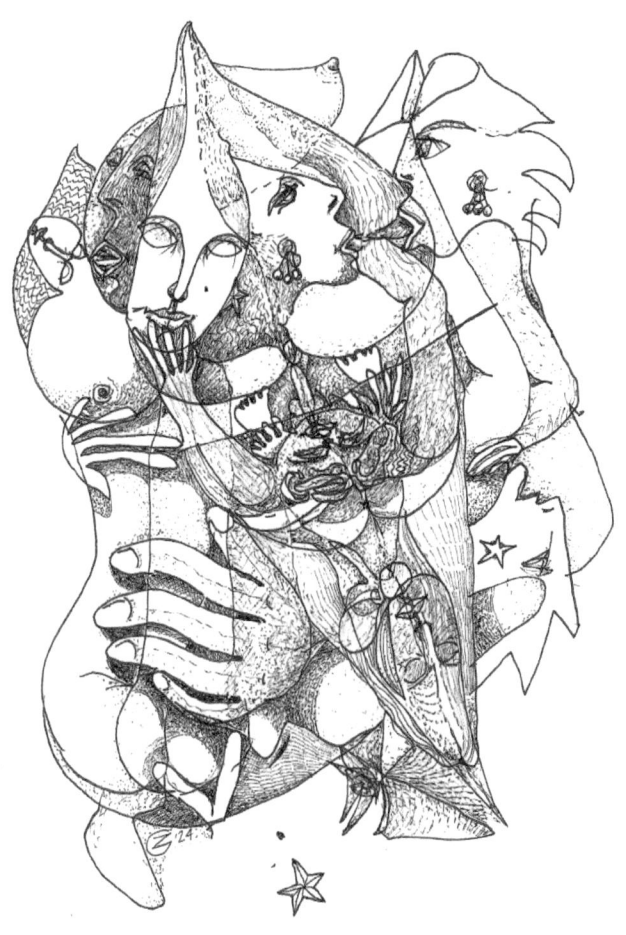

L&A II drwg. 33 (60) – enter paradise (day four)

in my first heat

at this beach, we go for a swim
h-mou and I, out to thalassa
to reach out to her is a desire
no water, no sun could quench
or burn, the salt of my body's juices
she stirs and I aim for the spot where
nobody could see us, or so we believe
as we kiss hot little kisses, never enough
greedy fingers grab her tits, squeeze her
breasts, in the sea's suspension we gasp
we interlock our thighs and my erection
wants to penetrate her to the rhythm of
the waves, the pushes of the sea. I want her.
I want her to be so aroused it feels like
hot flesh, my fingers on her I seek a back
position, but have to gasp and spit the
salty water that would drown me in my
lewd attempt, my cock strokes her vulva
but then how could we ever move together
reaching a climax, when drowning in the
sea of excitement demanding a greater
friction. ah! her womb is hot, her lips pursed
around my finger, I want her so badly I would
rip her apart, she would hold me between her
fingers, milking my cock, but it's too deep
down already out at the sea
to allow a fellatio and so I kiss her
in my first heat since I've arrived.

L&A II drwg. 34 (61) – in my first heat

into her heated body

a bronze man stands
in front of your door
frozen with shield and sword
the magpie screeches
evening isn't far away
and in the silence on the clouds
lustful love glows red
the longing of a long time
the arms strong and ready
to hold, to pull
her hips would open
receive me with wide-spread passion
that mixes with my constant urging
her murmurs that's like praying
and faster we ride, huddled together
entwined like plants in the inky sea
and oysters embrace her softness
pulling me deeper into the stronger sea
that separates, throws us and
only gives way to kissing
reaches like me for her
as I penetrate her most tender folds
finger deep into her heated body.

L&A II drwg 35 (62) – into her heated body

the meeting

    I went to the reception
sensing you'd come first to
greeting each other like a late
summer's breeze...
    thru' the plate glass doors
    I saw you moving up the
    marble steps and flung open
    one door leaf as if I'd entered
my other life, the one we've led
in secret for some time
now with a hug and some kisses
to the cheeks to finally seal it.
    the warmth of it glowed
    on both our faces
    the beat of our hearts shook up
    the minds of our spouses
all smiles you conversed with bee
while I endured the scrutiny of your
spouse, the man who loves
military parades, an iron fist to rule
to put his country back to the top
of the world.
    we smile exchanging pleasantries
    I learn the greek way of conversation
    Talking with hands and body language
emphasizing a point of view.

L&A II drwg 36 (63) – the meeting

thalassa

finally the day is fair
the sea at ebb
you take us to the beach you use
nearby, show your body
in a tight bikini
the dance of flesh that fires up
desire, the cooling waves
that hide the touches underwater
intimate and longing, pushed by
the waves throwing us together
further from ashore
as if poseidon would assist to let us
copulate with our bodies in suspension
impossible if one does not wish to drown
finger in your vulva for a few seconds
welcome in its heat like a hot ring
around my finger
while your fingers clasp my erection
trunks pulled down stretching supine
towards you, I pull your legs, we kiss
a fondling swim, moments of great desire
seawater's salt throws pebbles at us
as if this innocent float will disintegrate
dissolve, and we'll land up on the bottom
of this gulf thru' the powers of thalassa.

L&A II drwg 37 (64) - thalassa

you and I

if you think I am your man
fun diving in the sea
lust-chasing on land
hiding between the waves
touching below the blue
when trunks and tops skid off
in a wash
leaving you exposed
to my salty touch.
if you think I'm your lover man
you bend upon for lust and love
like a frightened deer with
glazed-over eyes seen in fright
until we hunt for lust
we cannot give way to our want
we cannot stretch for lack of a bed
if you think we still could
we'll be blessed with love that's
unusual and seen as a gift from all
who love, from all who have suffered
stealthy love and praised all lovers
like you praise me
like I praise you
oh here you are...
a bedtime story
you and I.

L&A II drwg 38 (65) – you and i

arrows

you wake me at five
each morning in the heat
of love or so I live now
perched as a dove on the
hot tin roof of illusions
I'm ready for your touches
your greedy lips
your furnace of a mouth
that swallows me like a log
of wood to burn in lust's cinder
you hold my chest and
pull my heart in a passion's fire
burning me into immortality
like achill
but for the purple spot
on my heart.
I hold your breast and feed
of its nipple like baby eros
feeds on Aphrodite
and play with the arrows
that pierced our hearts.

L&A II drwg 39 (66) - arrows

your sensuality

   your sensuality like mine
your mouth opens like a plant
a cup for a love potion
   your finger curls around
my erection like vines grasp
a wooden pole
   today you still want me
who knows what the morrow'
brings to the sand-filled shore.
   your sensuality like mine
your lips like a flower open up
a beaker for a love potion's sip.
   today I still love you
and long for warmth
shape you like leaves
create the heavenly child
who blows away your clothes.
   what does it mean to be
   in love but constant loving
   a play of sweet little things
   and waiting for the inner twang
   the rise and fall
   the penetrating call.

L&A II drwg 40 (67) – your sensuality

symposium

   every night some mysterious
flight of birds without feathers
and tesserae, smooth like pebbles
   a long-fingered hand or tracts
   from the body of a hetera
or is it that in this symposium
there is one man only and three
women of different stages of life
   and another man joins in to
   venerate the offspring of three
   more women
   she gives birth to two who spring
   from her stretched out body
   fully fledged and ready for an
orgy if you call it symposium
whatever – there's the intimate
togetherness of swung out bodies
that interlink and lie in folded
intricate patterns
   that roll and change in continual
   manner, at times a bird's face emerging
   at times a reptile, a curious fish
   with wavy hair between open fingers
with hair that curls around a nipple
and upside down lips touch
tongues flicker between fingers, faces
breasts and bums and nobody is
separated as all become a ball of one.

L&A II drwg.41 (68) - symposium

when I wake

while you are gone someplace
resembling sun and lake
I'm left with a cold bed
an empty tea cup black and silver
evaporated dreams
that lie strewn about and
gasp for we've been once close
and with a wanton feel.
montblanc pen, black shaft
orange book III *aphrodite encumbered*
its floral power stirred my senses
blood-red a lamy pen draws attention
dark green to it, naked as if bodies,
a parker pen touched once
by a muse's fingers, next to a journal
black and moleskine-slim, an aesthetic
alternative to writing
faber-castell the silver knight pen
that writes first time
I put it to a drawing test and its
smooth shaft that feels like my own
I miss to be touched by you
when I wake.

L&A II drwg.42 (69) – when I wake

let me tell you

let me tell you
how love swings us to
become children inside
    you turn much faster
into the sweet young child
than I, who admires your
charm, your beguiling smile
that has me mesmerized
    you shield your breast
and are conscious of your
nakedness, while I smile
admiring your lithe body of
a child turning into a woman
    and I take your hand
you feel wanted and trusted
we walk along beaten paths
thru' many centuries, people
who moved along before us
    then you come and ask me to
shed my clothes and be as naked
as you, hugging me and press
your sinewy body into mine
share the leap of heat as we
embrace
    let me tell you how love
will swing in us to become
children inside

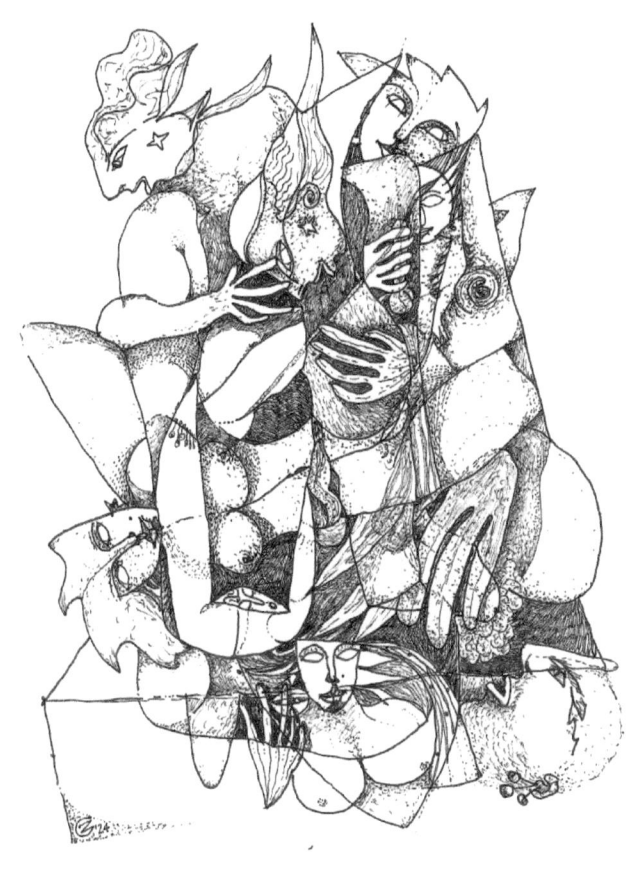

L&A II drwg 43 (70) – let me tell you

voyeur

wrestling with the man
at night who twisted my arm
  and pulled my tendon
it is you I rather wrestle with
  than a monster of my fantasies
or is it a bad sign of an inevitable
  change that'll push us
tan-skinned, but still too white
  for the sun's aggression
to the north?
  to arcadia to a poet's final burn
consumed by death's all-consuming
  love? and we celebrated with
touches on our bodies denuded
  from layers of restrictions
your mind that makes me grow
  is my mind opening you up
for me in this play of skin to skin
  responsive to a touch akin
a tongued flick lick desires catch
  on all these fires and passion
will visit our bed all night as the
  lecherous voyeur
who's part of our threesome.

L&A II drwg 44 (71) - voyeur

butterflies

    into a triangle of day's
happening with my hands
I shape your stretched out
    body and arms restricted
    legs pulled wide apart
the dough of life lies in great
moments of a sudden change
    life's intensity bursts from
    crystal configurations of our
world's angle
once inflicted upon us
    and in the meltdown
    of heat emanating out
    of our pores
    the flow of juices highlights
    the path our desires will be
guided by laser beams
from our organic-shaped
heart –
we pull and mould this
new creation out of the angulated
cocoon into the life of pre-set
butterflies
to let them fly
to let them fly.

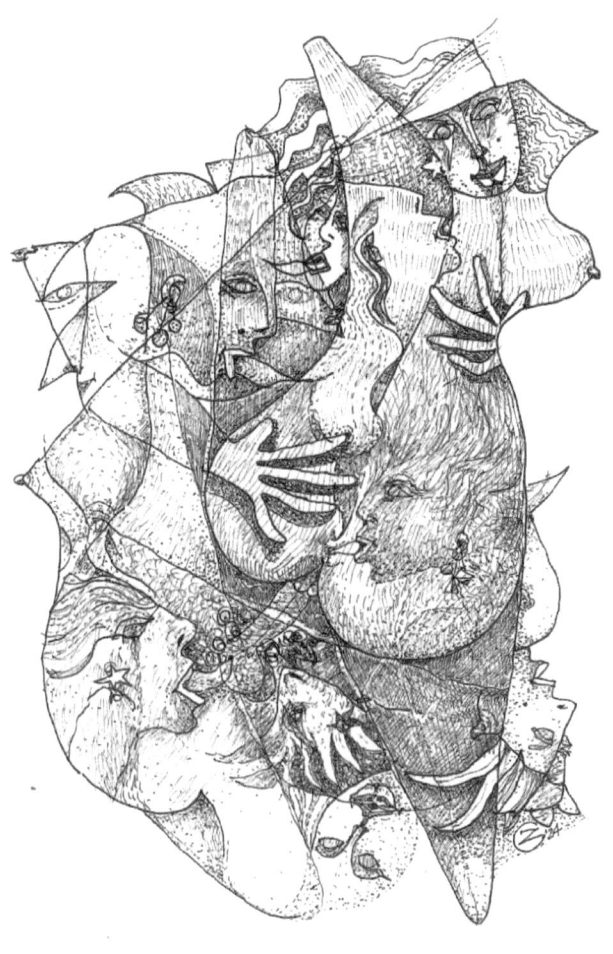

L&A II drwg 45 (72) - butterflies

another muse

touching my flailing
penis' crown and feel
like an old man
his desire still there
half moon, half hard
and I pull in desperation
to revive a flailing cock
whose cock, yours or mine?
whose hardness is it? the
new man's in your life?
or is it mine you've never
felt, you've never taken time
to unfold and caress?
the day you wanted to do it
the way you said it'll satisfy you
now I'm hard and can feel it
filling my hand
throbbing at my strokes
you'll miss out my love
tonight
another muse
will claim my juices.

L&A II drwg. 46 (73) – another muse

friendship

    into the eye of an african storm
hard and harsh like ice and thorn
I escape
a hermit crab
    who peeks out the window
    from my study's shell
e-hermes rings the bell
another letter
but this time unexpected
    like a cloudless day
    in summer
you'll still take up
your conversation
where emotions cut the thread
of friendship in bohemian anger
    artist's world that hardly changes
    has picked up sketches
    on the sea of faces
that reeled off the canvas
as fallen leaves
a lifeline of communication
a hand extended
a face so warm to clasp
    the human soul to embrace
    feelings that have never
    entirely faded

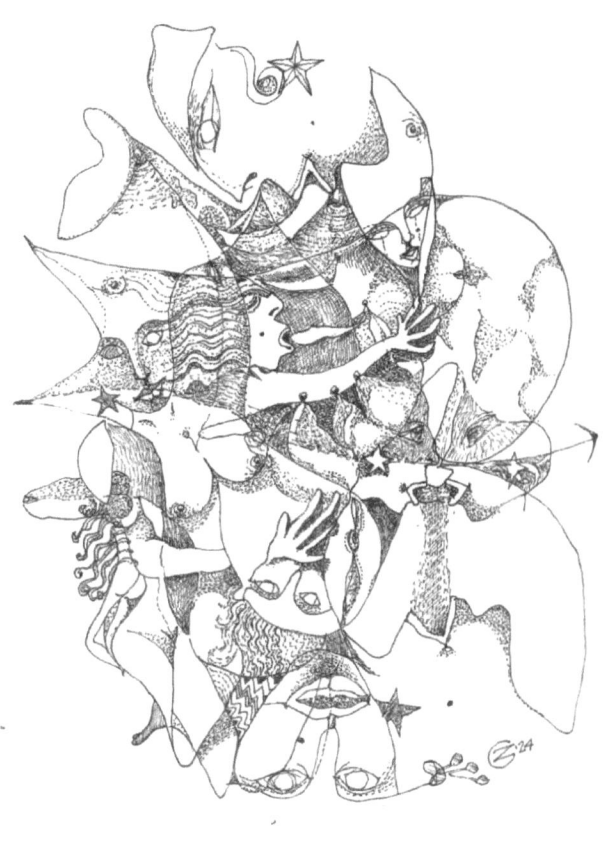

L&A II drwg.47 (74) - friendship

love & death

love lives next to death
or because of it
the bony fingers support
its smooth sister
stirring deep in her
an incestuous passion
embraced
thought of as an eternal enemy
in a duality with the cross
and the devil's face
with clean images of shells
modelled in the minds of
extortionists
where all's dead with
mechanical repetitions
love exists with death as a
doses of an everyday drug
for dying little by little
so the transition from life
isn't a shock
but a last and all-embracing
ecstasy.

L&A II drwg.48 (75) – love & death

in passionate lover's style

I sensed your message
lying down on my crumpled bed:
pegasus will bring me to you...
I recline and wait for your body
to stretch over mine
your hands touch me
stroke me into a mood for love
I'll join you in this overture
of a highway to heaven
oh, you are so good in these
physical acrobatics
or is it the soul that lifts from .
our bodies to dance the dance of
seven veils in front of our eyes
do we invite the lass for a
threesome?
there's no need for jealousy
with eyes closed it's the mind
that paints pictures of lewd desires
of the taboos, we are about to
transgress in a passionate
lover's style.

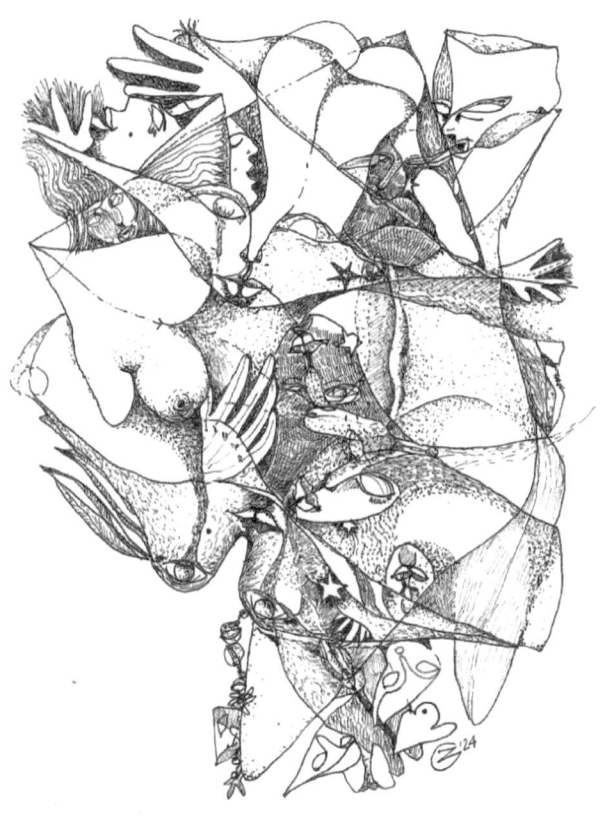

L&A II drwg.49 (76) – in a passionate lover's style

whirring wings

the conscious mind
like the first light shatters
the dreams of one night in love
I feel my morning's erection
I cherish like a jewel with love
as done for everyone by every
lady who enjoys the world of eros
and is in good luck of a matching
soul and mind
the body that is in sync with
your own.
I close my eyes and think of you
Your sweet smile, your body glow
The way you slide down your gown
Your generous breasts that
I devour
your lips that fold around
my crown in our oral love
where mouth and tongue
slip back and forth
bodies seek to absorb
and be absorbed
skin fuses with skin
in desire's heat, we give
ourselves in to
one soul with
whirring wings.

L&A II drwg.50 (77) – whirring wings

love's all around you

you talk of yesterday
the people pulling down
the berlin wall
your daughter in her crib
where she'd need lots of
courage to grow up in a majority
of dark people
you would not flee?
in some transformations
you talk about another friend
another love
and the dark-haired woman
from the periphery of angst
is a sushi lover and she'd tell you
the right way to sample ginger
with Japanese horseradish
and fresh fish, while you think
of having to throw in your believes
of the rainbow nation...
impossible to integrate a square
peg into a round hole or vice versa
while your friend smiles
selling your novel to his new girlfriend
you smile as love is all around you
you can feel it, sense it, and you
give it to your muse in cologne
where your past is buried
below the grand dome.

L&A II drwg.51 (78) – love's all around you

the poet's nine muses

  sent by my first fierce loving muse
who taught me the secret rites with her courageous
step into the 'big void'. their minds and bodies
  gravitate towards me: svety, the dusky voiced
  amazon from yerewan, deep-seated lust deep seated
in her womb; britty, the skin deep float of existence, bored
to death by conventions, but of stealthy staunchness
holding up her denuded breasts fighting for freedom;
  agi, the explosive gold coloured bubbling champagne
  woman, will she never drink it with me together?
  elena, the sapphire eyed woman from Belarus digging
the stone, transforming mountains, reshaping the world
and the minds, a torch in the icy darkness, with such
passion and deep feelings;
jo, aphrodite encumbered forever in lustful play with eros
  and ares, Adonis, and Priapus, most gentle loving
  soulmate and lover, and lina, her opposite elfin nymph
  from the woods of russia; simchi, who came in from
  the dream of life, once creating a a life of a dream that
resurfaced; sola, the dancing tamil lass who transformed
from mother to lover, from the muse of a poet to the
heroine of a novel by the poet most successful book.
In summary, here are the poet's nine muses::
svety, britty, agi, anne, elena, jo, lina, simchi, and sola
  and all nine have done, or will do
  have loved the poet, or still want to love him
  and will live in all the poet's books forever.

L&A II drwg.52 (79) – the poet's nine muses

blue moon

we met in many moons
it must be sixteen by now
and today for the seventeenth time
the one you called 'blue moon' and
set my mind off on a curious trail
following a chain of expressive talk
sweet memories of loves
patches of faces emblazoned on a
silver shield, meandering thoughts
on a warrior shield of great heroes
memories like a running wave pattern
flying off at revolving speed
of one full year now gone and wishes
flown to the heavens
captivating stars and planets.
in all the zillion of meetings, chats, and
get together I still find you with your
smile, can still dive into your eyes
still hold you tight, still caress you on
sight
will we meet on a full moon
sitting down at the great temple
that still shines bright on the
acropolis?

L&A II drwg.53 (80) – blue moon

tonight

    tonight I feel I've been
swept away by a torrential rain
the cry of unlimited tears
    strong vibes of the universe
    have pulled me away from you
made me suffer an uneven beating
heart, images of pain and bodies
stretching into the endless space
    reaching for the blue moon's
    waning rays
    that render power to the
    forces of the night
and some dear friends
are no more
and some beloved have sighed
a distant gasp
    into the wind's ear
    purple flight you come
    on this white horse
this cool affair
heating between
the dark sheets
of the flowing night's
sea of sweet togetherness.

L&A II drwg. 54 (81) – tonight

heavenly bodies

    feelings left loose between
the late night and early morn'
surges of a flight
by the white winged mare of fable
whose wings swing effortlessly
thru' the night sky's dreams
    you catch the dreams in
the net of your dusky hair
that floats along the milky way
bridge of lovers
fold of linen bedding
all whoever loved in the gardens
of andromeda
    my dreams circle like stars
around your smile, cool like rays
bouncing off the passing planets
you've visited with pegasus.
in the big wheel of fate
pluto shines and the chain of
heavenly bodies seek each other
reborn every night.

L&A II drwg. 55 (82) – heavenly bodies

litchi gland

    will you play with me
place your fingers around my
    crotch, fit snuggly with gentle
movements around your thumb
on my resting penis, let the twin balls
    roll in the bowl of your palm
    squeeze peon alive with love
    and care! Raise him from death
like lazarus, drop his mummification
extract the pink crown of life
taste its litchi gland for lust is a fruit
    and lust is berry pomegranate juice
    manna of the gods and honeysuckle
    in the garden of pleasures lies eros
    still who had an eternal childhood
growing up to taste your knobs of love
your mound of venus
your luscious breasts
in a coitus mammilla
a giant sliding act
    when the heavens tumble
    mountains shake and
    piercing swords are tonguing
    in a feast of never-ending love.

L&A II drwg. 56 (83) – litchi gland

erotic shards

you show me your dream
of pleasures that are present
in your erotic dream
fingers ten and five turn into
figures, faces, and erotic shards
lips will independently pursue
to still their hunger
arms like giant phalluses follow
hands extending into derrieres
shapely stretched, voile cloth
sliding down your leg
tongues feed us from the covers
giant licks that drive our libidos
up the wall in the box of
stealthy love, enhancer of our
minds in the erotic land
impenetrable by uninvited guests
who all want to be part of the
other life that is given
to the blessed
by aphrodite
and roused by eros.

L&A II drwg. 57 (84) – erotic shards

erotic symphony

while dreams pull me up
and your face races thru'
my blood eros brakes up
this cube, this pyramid of
the dark deep underworld
that imprisons the lustful
jouissance that cannot rise
in joy like a fluttering bird
caught in the twisting vines
and leaves, it turns into
our body parts and grows
to a tropical forest of gaping
flowers, budding stems that
gasp in a playful merging to
a cacophony of a bird's
orchestral warble, a music of
the senses in a rising dawn
when fingers penetrate each
other's flesh, like predators
feasting on prometheus' liver
the manna from the heavens
flowing freely from another
night's erotic symphony.

L&A II drwg. 58 (85) – erotic symphony

jouissance

you have a longing in
your heart that matches mine
even at great distances across
sinai and the red sea that reaches
the horn of africa

across the med's shimmer of blue
to the pyramids of giza and following
along the nile down to cross its source
towards the dark lands of southern africa
I sail stretched out like dionysus in my
freedom's boat with grapes below its
bowing sail.

and you are close to me
much closer than anybody could imagine
be it in the corner pub or ambling with me
familiar exercising paths
you'll fetch me for a têtê-á-têtê.

the other afternoon you came around
an angel I'd been waiting for a long time
a prophecy I thought I'd heard before
at the spot in delphi, some time ago.

you squat below my writer's desk
open my pants for an intimate caress
seducing me with your specific style.

I have such a great appetite for
writing about you that I will do it, while
being in your mouth, your face,
your cheeks, your denuded neck
I douse in jouissance.

L&A II drwg. 59 (86) – jouissance

I draw a picture

I draw a whole book like others
swallow their draughts
I love your quim as others dig
In the ground to find an elusive gem
get rich on one diamond
I draw a picture of your face in love
when my fingers close around your
breast and play with your nipple's knob
the bell to enter your door to
enormous sensual riches:
rubies of lust, sapphire eyes,
the pearls of excitement
the sole decoration on your skin I collect
and you sigh
as I dive down deep between
the coral reefs
and breathe new life
into the fins that rise and
pop up their bowing sails
I draw your body
as one with mine.

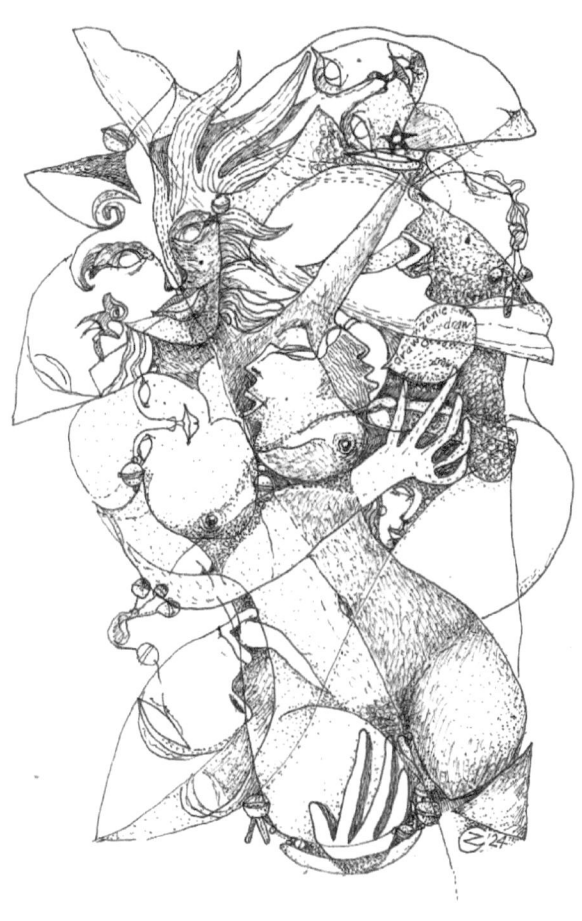

L&A II drwg.60 (87) – I draw a picture

ghosts of the past (1)

    ghosts of the past haunt me
that came from an ice-white sky
a barrage of hail hammered on
my roof paining me with visions
I had forgotten a long time ago:

    the dark-haired woman from
yerewan walking like a living dead
her lungs wheezing with every word
her eyes glowing in feverish glances

    the small-chested mish who
entrusted me to pierce her hymen
that felt not like a piercing, but rather
like a very tight fit and more like a
rape, she still pains my soul asking
for love she never found.

    a pursed-lipped chrissie, soft
buxomed and sensuous, even in
petting she exuded deep desires
spiralled me up into great lust
without a penetration, she feared
for a pregnancy, forbidden by
strict religious code.

    not to mention karen, who
wished to make oral love, but had
no experience yet and we made it
just fine with the pain of biting into
delicious flesh in great lust
wonder if she did it again.

L&A II drwg.61 (88) – ghosts of the past p 1

ghosts of the past (2)

to a lucky fella
    her sister-in-name, actress, and
dancer wished to keep her virginity
and left us, two friends at a task to
play our cocks at her vaginal entrance
gate, but teasing us to ejaculate
over her entire body.
    wonder if she has now children
or if she is a theatre nut and life has
turned out for her as she wished?
    are we all plagued by our ghosts
of the past
or is it the bard who alone
has to suffer on lonely nights?

L&A II drwg.62 (89) – ghosts of the past p 2

your greatest slide show

    perched on the disk of a
blue moon
like a white dove, you tempt me
with your drawn-out limbs
that accommodate an illustrious
highway of the great erotic:
e three-faced symposium below
a great quim that opens to
swallow them up
a hermaphrodite with an upside
down demeanour
an angel stripped, denuded
who fell into the sweet trap
of great lust
spreading her lissom legs
perpendicular around a wizard
ghost and a busker
who plays an array of instruments
to a great celestial dance
    will you change like the
planet earth, dunked into blue
light
and play your greatest slide show
of instant merging
until the first crack of light?

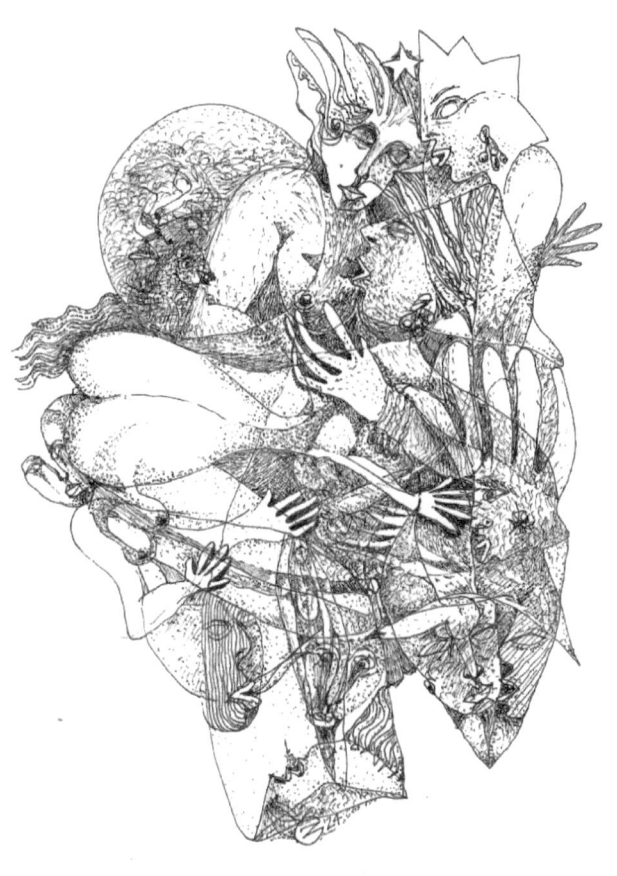

L&A II drwg.63 (90) – your greatest slide show

for a long time now

    face to face the kissing
    that entices the woman
in you and from her springs the
other you: the full-breasted
aphrodite who loves the woman
whose exposed derriere she strokes
her statue she'll bring to a
life-assembled gathering for
a têtê-á-têtê.
    breast to breast, face to body
embraces and more embraces
lips to breasts and tongues to
thighs, the lover who holds you
tightly playing with your hardened
nipples stretches into you.
    it might be your past lover
your ghost of love you stretch into
as many hands long to touch you
as many lips play on you
many tongues adore your skin
    but once you long for one
    penetration you bend down for
    the one you have wanted
    for a long time now.

L&A II drwg.64 (91) – for a long time now

every night

    every night comes rain
come moonlight's cool shine
you descend from the heavens
compliments of pegasus' airy
white horse you could take
anywhere
    pull the sheets of black silk
with a red dragon's head across
the bed in the clouds where a
celebration will be held at full moon
the pan world orchestra entertains
with music of the spheres:
vivaldi, mozart, schubert, beethoven
and berg, shostakovitsch
we dance to the tango appassionata
from astor piazzola in the bed of the
foam of paradise, shaped by our bodies.
    every night thru' to the crack of dawn's
blue light reflections of the med's sea
drops of dew-like faces from life's
collection.

L&A II drwg.65 (92) – every night

bodies made of marble

   welcome to my room
freshly painted white walls
cream wood, lacquer mirrors
over the bed and further at
its wide end
for you to see me
for me to see the angles we
wish to recall time and time
again
   I paint the scenes into the
square white tiles that cover the
suspended floor
your portrait, your nude
your body parts, your breasts
my hands, your hands, and my
pleasant erection
that you call up magically
every time
   besides an assembly of birds
and heads of muses with wings
bodies made of marble.

L&A II drwg.66 (93) – bodies made of marble

a flashfire surge

the ghosts that follow me –
fire-headed corpus ithyphallic
a bevy of beautiful women
bodies luscious like ripe fruit
the curtains of time lifted
exposing the bodies behind
pale, shrunk, like toys
spider web to the touch
shattered shards of glass
I cut my soul within
you came from the lush-leafed
garden like a dream and cooled
my heated wounds with a shower
of touches, cooking me like
lamb stew
I licked you like strawberry and
whipped cream
desert in love is what counts
in the end
desert is the swollen lip that
burns in the heavenly juices
you offer me with your body
split into two
and paradise licks us up
in a flashfire surge.

L&A II drwg.67 (94) – a flash fire surge

piercing and become
pierced

   at twenty past-five
when the sounds of a
haydn symphony is echoed
by the warbling birds outside
   your touches wake me
gently and with a fire in your
heart you want me
that it flashes in me repeatedly
like a tzaki on a cold morning's
embrace we fire away like in
love's sweet battle of cinnamon
honey, nuts, and yourti
   far away from travels in outer
space we find each other continuously
searching for another climb
another spiral's screw
an all-encompassing clasp
an even tighter hug
   I have you often and like in
love's merging
we change places piercing
and become pierced.

L&A II drwg.68 (95) – piercing and becoming pierced

sleeping doll

she lives high up in the
clouds above the city that
slowly wakes up to seek their
treasures and their sanctuaries
the real treasures
and he hides her from the
public eye, the men who look at her
the occasional lover who sneaks up
to her when cereberus is asleep
when the time is ripe for a têtê-á-têtê
a grab and run, a quickie enticing
by its stealthy nature.
he found her asleep, a sleeping
doll, he dug from the city's debris
like aphrodite's shards, he placed
together and prayed to the goddess
of love to listen to the words of
a bard.
in a short time she was alive and
well on her way mended by his kisses
his touches and the love he placed
along her encumbered body parts.

L&A II drwg.69 (96) – sleeping doll

tighter caress

I can feel you – se niatho –
I have this itch and arousal in
the middle of the night
under the shower
in front of the pc
whenever I see a naked body
that resembles you.
these are all muses
but in the end, they all lead
to you and morph into your
face, your smile, your body,
your lust, your pleasure.
I can feel your fingers
stroking me and playing with
my nipples and my cock you
clasp, place your lips upon
the sucking makes me hard.
your warmth I feel from
head to breast and pussy
thighs and deep in you for
a great dip and come, then
a dig into your behind that
crowns the loving with a final
tighter caress.

L&A II drwg.70 (97) – tighter caress

I would burn you

  I would place you
Into the furnace of love
I would burn you
never bury you
but before all that
I would hug you, commit
an act of necrophilia
and love you
before the fires would
consume you
before my spunk is buried deep
in you
then with emotions flaming highs
I burn like you but on the inside
take the silver urn up to the
sacred rock, I stand high on the
south-western wall and let you fly
into the aeolus, my arms marking
the spot where I wanted to fly off
as well, before you, who knows?
the game is open and it'll change
to the tune of fate's toughest
women, but it's our secret for evol
besides for those who have a
heart.

L&A II drwg.71 (98) – I would burn you

angel

angel of sweetness like a white
cloud on a dark angry night
like a sail of pristine white
on a stirred-up ink pot of sea
have you forfeited your love
that once you made me set the boat
of freedom escaping the dark-pointed
fingers of a night sky that turned
its clouds against the righteous folk
the humble poet, the honest writer
of words that are shields of Achilles
and Athena to save the lonely bard
from being lanced by dusky
perpetrators

L&A II drwg.72 (99) - angel

Towards the calm of the Med

Est-ce avoir l'air musician
que d'avoir l'air des villes?
I'm not looking like a musician
rather like a poet, a messenger
of words my Muse whispers
and you asked if I'm at ease
in cities?
It seems so. I'm used to it now
after lifelong conditioning and
painful transformations
completely unnatural
like the golf swing.
It has hurt my mind like a draw
that sends me between stirred-up
drivers of enormous trucks
as if everybody would be in transport
shoving sand for gold
turning the steppe upside down
for the one big diamond.
I will flee the dust that descends
down as soot with thunderstorms
I will leave the land of darkness
that obliterated the rainbow of its
prospective harmonies
I'll put my life on a boat, pray to Poseidon
we'll pass the Horn of Africa towards
the calm of the Med, the Mediterranean Sea
without being held up for ransom.

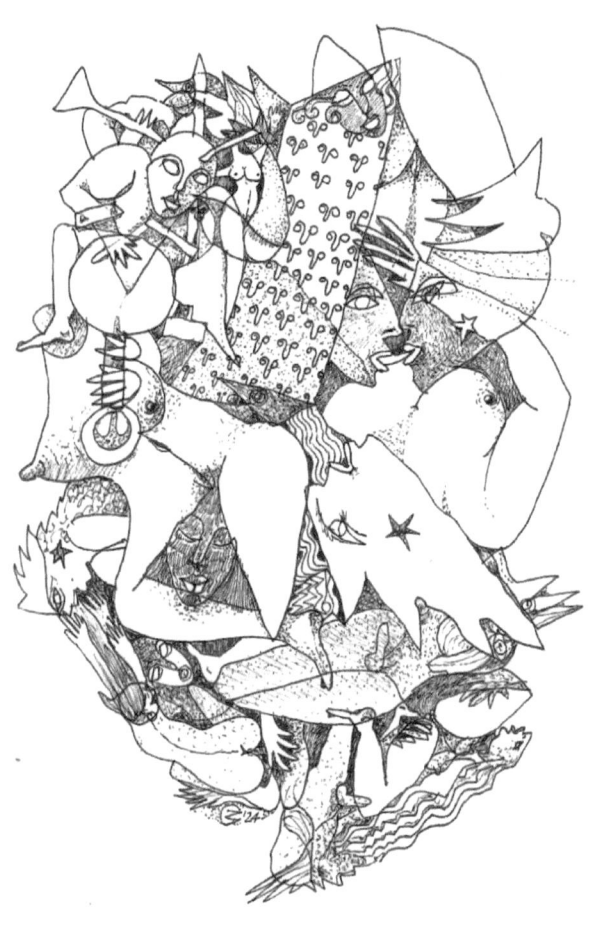

L&A II drwg.73 (100) – towards the calm of the Med

at the crack of dawn

in the shadows of the night
you meet her like a thief
having stolen her heart.
In the darkness of the night
you love her, but first light will
come fast.
Stealthy love is exciting
the spice of life and the purpose
of your existence
that transferred into her for
betterment of her fragile being
that she rules with a strong mind.
at the crack of dawn when lying
together is most loving and sweet
she has to go for fear of him waking
and holding the club of words
to strike her down
pulling the knife of hate that once
had been love
deny her unbridled he cannot give
or enjoy any longer.
But she's stronger every time
And Aphrodite protects her from
A deranged spouse.

L&A II drwg.74 (101) – at the crack of dawn

a pleasure's thorn

   I'm lost since you have
turned around while the moon
showed its waning crescent
   the world turned to the
inclemency of an angry god
   all's cold and damp
besides, my stomach rumbles
songs of yesteryear
   as I read Khajjam's strophes
of love's thrashing floor, my balls
feel punished by hard squeezing
   my cock pulled by the vehement
hand of violent times, when you
disappeared into the Attic mist.
   I've no doubts, but watch the clouds
to burst and let you free. I pray,
even adore the cusp of the moon
that looks to me like
a pleasure's thorn.

L&A II drwg.75 (102) – a pleasure's thorn

togetherness

you do not ask me for
turning my webcam on
even in a state of horny
togetherness.
I wait until you are confident
and you'll do it, just being so sexy
when you watch me masturbating
for you, you say and do yourself...
I see you coming when I bend down
from my elevated stay, as I can only
do it standing up; cannot lie down
I have no bed in my studio, no linen
no cosiness, no softness to lie upon
and we could be two lovers
like in the book, 'Izane has the thrift',
makes us to become lovers forever.

L&A II drwg.76 (103) - togetherness

voluptuous beauty

what do I compose with you
in mind – a floating scene
of nudes and body penetrations
a dismembered body part
hands folding around the
voluptuous body of a woman
while her carapace folds into
another woman's derriere
a face of sadness doused with tears
an upside-down of participants
you would say 69, and I would say
it is the natural folding and unfolding
of legs and hands
the continuous change of
perspectives: yours, mine,
your girlfriend's
my poet's face,
my face as a man and
buccaneer, an intruder,
and a ravisher of your
voluptuous beauty.

L&A II drwg.77 (104) – voluptuous beauty

I fall

In the middle of the night
the skies fell on me
the heavens storm-whipped
like an angry sea
you cried out for an axe
the main mast of the ship
in fear of splitting your head
the crackling of the skies
an earth turned upside down
rolling in the bed of a heaving
up and down
until you fall out
cover your head
cover your nape with your hands
someone called the triangle of life
I always saw the tensions of eros
on the tip of his silver arrow
not Poseidon's anger
bodies shift against each other
and in our bodies,
we cower deeper
the mast of the ship into your
cries I fall.

L&A II drwg.78 (105) – I fall

cloud of possession

the cloud of possession
sweeps into the night
of my passion
desires are split up crystals
of a shattered viewing glass
my body dismembered
you seek to place it together
unfitting parts from the dark
path of body parts
that float in the sticky air
of abandoned loves
the junkyard of broken-up
tété-à-tétés and relationships
that drifted away into times
of indecision
a gap warms the primordial
composition for some life
to emerge
the triad of goddesses sweep
above the human lover
flakes of grand promising
creation their tongue
of stirring, ripping through
the denuded masses.

L&A II drwg.79 (106) – cloud of possession

rough ride

you wake me in the
wee hours of a dark morn.'
the melody of Yellow River
looms on my mind
are you sending me a reminder?
I have thoughts of love, not anger
life's still young for you
but for me, already a mature descend
into the world of dusky stillness
like this night when you are close,
yet a spirit, untouchable and distant
but so near.
friendship is a mutual
belonging of minds that can touch
as they used to
love, an adventure too often
losing the gardens of beauty
venturing into the darkness
to some unknown places
in a rough ride.

L&A II drwg. 80 (107) – rough ride

let's make love

    I miss your presence
your powerful erotic vibes
that have been disturbed
through political strife
and demonstrations
that turned violent
to vent people's anger
or are they paid for by the
opposition?
    to take a revolution to
the streets appeal to the
inexperienced 'Young Turks'
who spray paint the riot police
beat them with the throwing
of Molotov cocktails
hammer down shop windows
but who are those in their
black balaclavas?
Somebody said:
the known unknowns, aha!
Does it make sense?
No, violence in politics never do
unfortunately, Forget them
come, let's make love!

L&A II drwg. 81 (108) – let's make love

protective angel

It's 3h30 am, and the buzzer
at the entrance gate sounds
pressed by an emergency caller
  who's that so early in the mor'n?
someone looking for an asylum
or the preacher from next door
as the bell is pressed continuously
I'm up and stumble to the speaker
'Who is it?'
"Your gate is wide open," a man said
with a quiet and controlled voice.
  My god, I must have pressed the
wrong gate control by mistake again.
This happens in a cycle, I'm shocked.
The whole electrical fence of no use
with one silly button pressed
accidentally.
  I thank the man, but sleep had
eluded me by now.
'You must check in future at night
before we retire,' my spouse said.
indeed! I have to.
Thank you good angel
whoever sent you!

L&A II drwg. 82 (109) – protective angel

the spray of mist

   it's not the night
that is stirred up by
the deeds of lovers
crystalizing in the stars
   it's your mind that plays
a scherzo, a Webber tune
turning my being into
flotsam on a sea of emotions
   that settle on the beach
of quietude
where I palimpsest the
lifelines with my pen
placing paper like dropped
clothing between you and
the lapping of the waves –
ideas sailing the Med's blue
on top of its restless surface –
a canvas I paint upon
a mirror at dawn
that reflects your love
your nude cut-into half
by the keel of my composition
I sail, I sail!
The spray of mist that is you.

L&A II drwg. 83 (110) – the spray of mist

wings of eros

    I can't see you anymore
but can sense you still
cannot kiss you on the
electronic image
where I disrobed you
press myself against you.
    I can't see you any longer
at our daily tété-à-tété
but I'm ready for your mind
that strokes me with its wings
of eros
raising my cock, and playing
a song of love like a flute
between your lips
and in your mouth.
    I can feel your tongue
slicing me like cream cakes
apart in the early morning
tasting this new awakening
praying to the new
god of love.

L&A II drwg.84 (111) – wings of eros

erotic love

    she still lives in me
with her last words, I listened to
like a poet listens
who'll record unusual ways of love.
    she still touches me from
far away with her being
she slipped into my new Muse
or is she as old as I am
as old or young as she's ageless
but a name I've given her.
    she still appears at night
an apparition that turns into my
sexual love, we've always nurtured
together, my soul-mate, lover, friend
and sister with attitudes drawn from
all these avatars of the soul she lays
bare for me, and I live on by now.
    she still appears, but her words
are spoken thru' a Muse she has chosen
for me, a lover, I've responded to
a soulmate who grew out of it all
a woman of great sensual depth
she loves me, nourishing this
subterranean existence of erotic love.

L&A II drwg. 85 (112) – erotic love

human happiness

   my waking into a cold morning
with dreams turning into crystals
khim phoning words of romance
I had of her a generation back.
   the crystalized eros that melted in
her desire, she detected for a poet
in her family, kisses, touches, and
intimacy, she'll devour pursuance
of a trinity of personalities I did not
pay much attention to except for
a time when love had hurt me.
   at the present turning point of
living up to my stealthy love
when my personal life is balanced
around my muse, who balances her
libido spreading her feet to receive
my sexual being, aroused by cyber-shows
   all that desire of fusing flesh to flesh
and bone to bone, mixing our white blood
as the poetess noted, comes out to boil
in a narrow window-turning voyeur
for the gift of human happiness.

L&A II drwg. 86 (113) – human happiness

a heap of so many

   when a writer's icicle fingers pierce
my heart, I think of you so hard
that you'll come to push this red-hot
poker against a skeleton of ice
you hold it for a long time until it's
diving into you, singing your flesh
and it's my flesh, or whose flesh?
For I'm no longer dead when the desire
to embrace drives us over the edge
at mountains with bursts of rock.
   I'll be home all right from a generation
of years I've spent treading red clay
to shape the body of my muse, who
resided elsewhere
mocking my efforts to bag all the words
I could find along the trail of high seas
sailing along mountainous roads that
threw me off
   across the African continent, I would
return to bring back my beads of stories
I've spun but through another muse
her spirit, I've challenged, her body
a bag of bones
thrown at the heap of so many.

L&A II drwg. 87 (114) – a heap of so many

evasive soul

   she, the centre of his
body's shield he placed
before his soul
   or is it that in this heated
battle of love it would melt down
to one single mould
she places her fingers around
moulding it into a rod of great
heat and sensation
she plays like a flute
changes it with lips and tongue
reshaping all into a frenzy of
machine parts
pistons that slide into pink sheaths
at the speed of light
at slow delicious feasting of melon
pear, and pomegranate
with the urge of primordial haste
to be in all of her
opening up all orifices
searching for
her evasive soul.

L&A II drwg. 88 (115) – evasive soul

love & death

   I am drawing love and death
the way the crow flies, the way
it comes up in me, on a dead,
quiet morning
when my soul reflects on love
that has not been the usual
run-of-the-mill affair.
   I am letting my favourite
ink pen run freely across the
eggshell skin of paper rather
unforced enjoying the sound
of stroking you in love, my muse
of solitary hours.
   I am drawing love in bold
configurations in parts like an artist
places together his mosaic as it
comes at a random choice of all parts
as they are innate in my blood.
   I have drawn death, love's
pale shadow that followed me
for many years, but it might
withdraw now that you love me
every night, my muse,
Aphrodite-like, who never misses
the warmth of my bed.

L&A II drwg. 89 (116) – love & death

train of thoughts

train of thoughts
racing through the night
wheels of steel red-hot
grinding, pushing this energy
to limits far beyond the speed
dreams will appear
that cross the universe
passing all exciting places
revolving crystal balls of wondrous
shapes in quaintness
floating like suspended objects d'art
bubbles in conserving liquids
turning on a potter's wheel
reshaping by innate laws and
touches of the poet's pen
train of feelings with a life
of their own
reshaping your portrait
your body in the fading
starlight's dawning blue.

L&A II drwg. 90 (117) – train of thoughts

devil's eye

breast of pheasant
doe-eyed dove
I hold your chick-fear
quiver
in the palm of my hands
your soul walks at night
across the blue-dunked
globe
liquid gold's flow
rolling about mercury
from sheets of ice
thru murky seas
dark conspicuous pebble
of devil's eye
you guard with your spreading
thighs
your heaven's rosy glow
that pulls me into the
spiralling turn of the screen
of unbearable passion
soft-furred squirrel
firing me on
catching its slippery folds
all night.

L&A II drwg. 91 (118) – devil's eye

Index of poems and drawings

About the author

Born in eastern Austria, close to the Hungarian border, he witnessed as a young man the horrors of a nation's suppression, erupting in the Hungarian Revolution of 1956. He finished his education in art and architecture in Vienna, married, and sailed for the Cape of Africa, an adventure that followed his childhood dreams. He had drawn African animals for his art classes, but the time had come to see them in their natural habitat.

Meeting a varied facet of people and cultures, working as a draughtsman in an engineering office, and as an architect for a cultural centre, he made good use of his language skills travelling throughout Southern Africa.

During a trip to Lesotho, a native artist showed him rock paintings with their stark palimpsest outlines and with typified movements of animals and humans. It made a lasting impression on him and influenced his artistic work.

His vast collection of drawings and slides had been lost during a change of domiciles, but further studies of the San people would reawaken his dormant artistic longing for the expression of his art, filling sketchbooks with drawings and notepads with poetry and prose. While revisiting the capitals of Europe, he sensed that the bond of art being borderless and free, would reach across continents into the world. During a visit to Greece, he was accepted into a circle of artists and poets, who encouraged him to continue his art, and a poetess introduced him to the works of famous Greek poets.

In South Africa, he joined the writing and poetry workshops of *Writers Write*. It was to open the floodgates of his creativity. He decided to travel through Greece and visit its sites of antiquity, read up on Classical mythology, and enjoy first-class translations of Greek poetry and prose.

He settled in 2013/14 in Klosterneuburg-Weidling. Poet Nikolaus Lenau is buried here. Franz Kafka had visited here.
Their writings will always be an inspiration.

Other books by the author

(Available at BoD-Books on Demand/bookshop, Norderstedt, and at all major bookshops, as e-books or in print).

In English:

Acropolis – Book I. Fervour
Athens Elegies – A Poet's Lament
Cantos Libidos – Love's Pure Emotion
Clouds I – Dancing Eros
Clouds II – Wing-Child Eros
Diary of an Aged April – a month in the life of a poet on the
                    Southern hemisphere
Educating Pizzy – The Artist Evolves
Elegy of an Unusual Peak, Book I – Real and Virtual Loves
Elegy of an Unusual Peak, Book II – Days in Love
Fighting Stance – Triangulation in Love
King of Ice – A Poetic Legend
LOVE & ART – Songs of Passion, First Volume
MUSES – The artist between heaven and hell
MUSES II – The artist in the Muses' garden
MUSES III – Waking in Love
MUSES IV – Magic Unisons
Poetry in times of lockdowns and isolation, Book I –
                 Missing the City's Hub
Poetry in times of lockdowns and isolation. Book II –
                  The City Deserted
POETRY OF THE INNERMOST Book I – Colour Scales of Love
POETRY OF THE INNERMOST Book II –
                    In Praise of Mature Women
Red Tower Room – A Poet's Refuge
Short Stories Part 1 – From a Writer's Workshop
Short Stories Part 2 – Book III/IV
Short Stories Part 3 – Perpetual Eros
Spleen of Love – Zen and the Lake Moeris Adventure